My *Canada*
BRITISH COLUMBIA

By Sheila Yazdani

TABLE OF CONTENTS

A Crabtree Seedlings Book

Crabtree Publishing
crabtreebooks.com

School-to-Home Support for Caregivers and Teachers

This book helps children grow by letting them practice reading. Here are a few guiding questions to help the reader build his or her comprehension skills. Possible answers appear in red.

Before Reading:

• What do I know about British Columbia?
  • *I know that British Columbia is a province.*
  • *I know that British Columbia has many beaches.*

• What do I want to learn about British Columbia?
  • *I want to learn which famous people were born in British Columbia.*
  • *I want to learn what the provincial flag looks like.*

During Reading:

• What have I learned so far?
  • *I have learned that Victoria is the capital of British Columbia.*
  • *I have learned that Vancouver Island is the largest island on the Pacific coast of North America.*

• I wonder why...
  • *I wonder why the provincial flower is the Pacific dogwood.*
  • *I wonder why British Columbia grows so many blueberries.*

After Reading:

• What did I learn about British Columbia?
  • *I have learned that Vancouver is the largest city in British Columbia.*
  • *I have learned that the provincial animal is the Kermode bear.*

• Read the book again and look for the glossary words.
  • *I see the word **capital** on page 6, and the word **waterfalls** on page 16. The other glossary words are found on pages 22 and 23.*

2

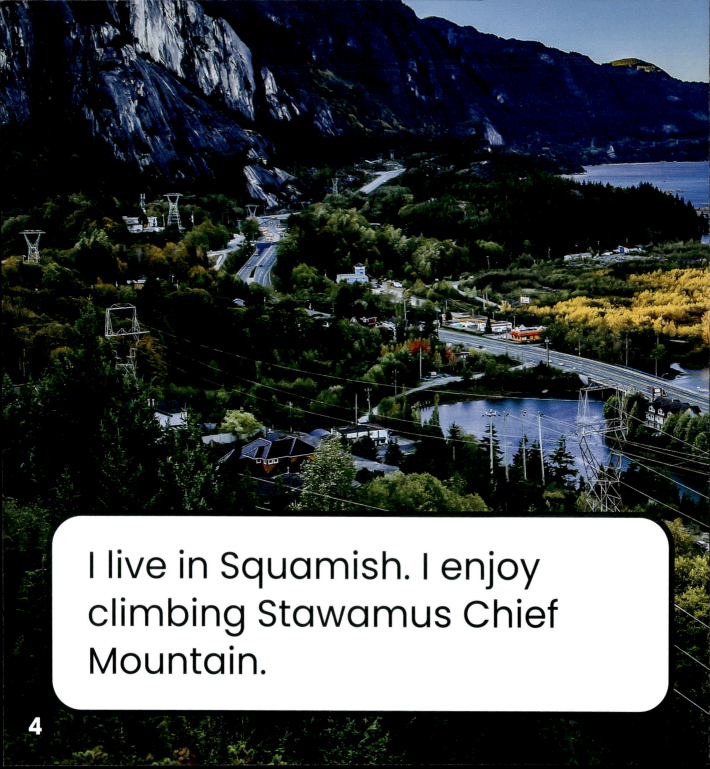

I live in Squamish. I enjoy climbing Stawamus Chief Mountain.

My town is known for its many fun outdoor activities, such as hiking, mountain biking, skiing, and more!

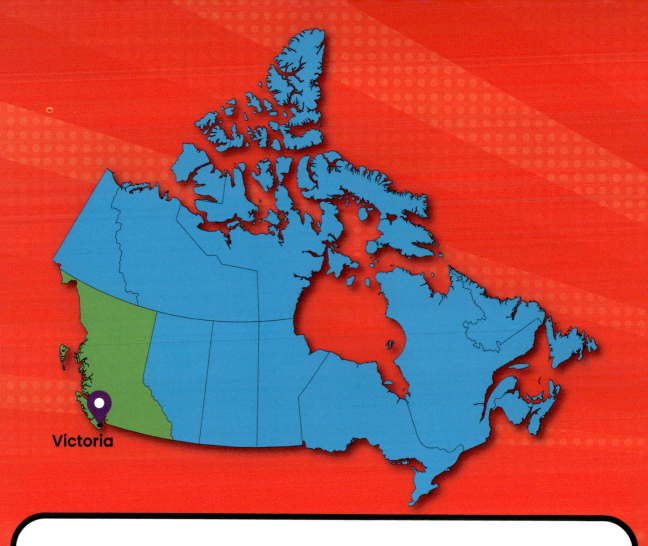

Victoria

British Columbia is a **province** in western Canada. The **capital** is Victoria.

Fun Fact: Vancouver is the largest city in British Columbia.

The provincial animal is the **Kermode bear**.

The Pacific dogwood is the provincial flower.

We grow a lot of blueberries in British Columbia. Some of them are used to make blueberry muffins.

Fun Fact: British Columbia grows around 90% of Canada's blueberries.

My provincial flag has a setting sun on it. Above the sun is a **Union Jack**.

My family likes to watch the Vancouver Whitecaps play soccer.

Fun Fact: Vancouver Island is the largest island on the Pacific coast of North America.

I enjoy seeing **waterfalls** at Yoho National Park.

I like to learn about history at Barkerville Historic Town and Park.

Voice actor Thomas Middleditch was born in British Columbia. NHL hockey player Shea Weber was also born in British Columbia.

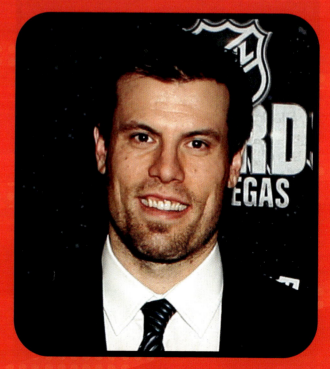

Fun Fact: Elsie MacGill, the first woman in the world to earn a degree in **aeronautical** engineering, was born in Vancouver, British Columbia.

My family enjoys canoeing on Okanagan Lake.

21

Glossary

aeronautical (air-uh-NOT-i-kuhl): Relating to the science of designing and building airplanes

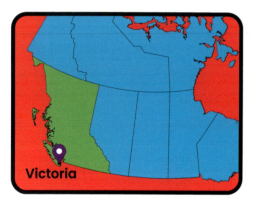

Victoria

capital (CAP-ih-tuhl): The city or town where the government of a country, state, or province is located

Kermode bear (ker-MOHD bayr): A type of bear that lives in the central and north coast regions of British Columbia

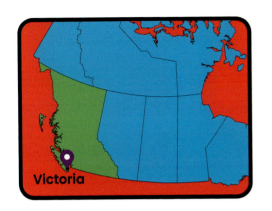

province (PROV-ins): One of the large areas that some countries, such as Canada, are divided into

Union Jack (YOON-yuhn jak): The flag of the United Kingdom

waterfall (WOT-er-fall): A natural stream of water that falls from a high place

Index

About the Author

Sheila Yazdani lives in Ontario near Niagara Falls with her dog Daisy. She likes to travel across Canada to learn about its history, people, and landscape. She loves to cook new dishes she learns about. Her favorite treat is Nanaimo bars.

Written by: Sheila Yazdani
Designed and Illustrated by: Bobbie Houser
Series Development: James Earley
Proofreader: Melissa Boyce
Educational Consultant: Marie Lemke M.Ed.

Photographs:
Library and Archives Canada: p. 19, 22
Newscom: Marc Sanchez/Icon SMI 144: p. 18 right
Shutterstock: Harry Beugelink: cover; 2009fotofriends: p. 3; Ludmila Ruzickova: p. 4-5; Media Guru: p. 6, 22-23; f11photo: p. 7; Lynn A: p. 8, 22; John Yunker: p. 9; Bryan Pollard: p. 10-11; Krasula: p. 11; Steve Allen: p. 12, 23; lev radin: p. 13; Russ Heinl: p. 14; Neil Podoll: p. 14-15; Scott Bennie: p. 16, 23; Vicki L. Miller: p. 17; Kathy Hutchins: p. 18 left; Elena_Alex_Ferns: p. 20; Fremme: p. 21

Crabtree Publishing

crabtreebooks.com   800-387-7650
Copyright © 2025 Crabtree Publishing

Printed in the USA/062024/CG20240201

Published in Canada
Crabtree Publishing
616 Welland Avenue
St. Catharines, Ontario
L2M 5V6

Published in the United States
Crabtree Publishing
347 Fifth Avenue
Suite 1402-145
New York, New York, 10016

Library and Archives Canada Cataloguing in Publication
Available at Library and Archives Canada

Library of Congress Cataloging-in-Publication Data
Available at the Library of Congress

Hardcover: 978-1-0398-3851-2
Paperback: 978-1-0398-3936-6
Ebook (pdf): 978-1-0398-4017-1
Epub: 978-1-0398-4089-8